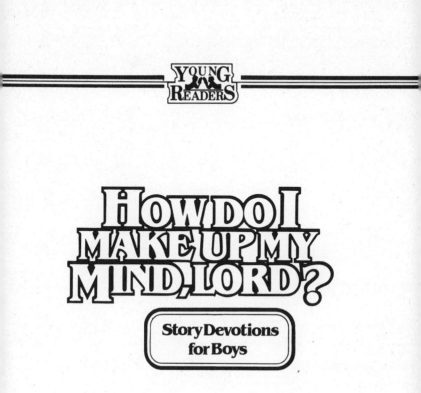

HOW DO I MAKE UP MY MIND, LORD?

Story Devotions for Boys

ROBERT KELLY

AUGSBURG Publishing House • Minneapolis

HOW DO I MAKE UP MY MIND, LORD?

Illustrations by Tom Maakestad.

Contents

About This Book

How often have you said to yourself, "I've got to make up my mind!"? You are faced with a decision or a problem that must be solved. You need help. Where do you find it? Sometimes from parents or friends. Talking it out with them can help.

When you read these stories you will discover they are about boys just like you, with problems just like yours. They want to be accepted by their classmates, make the team, win at competition, feel good about themselves. Sometimes they are afraid, sometimes they are angry, sometimes they are heroes. You will also discover something else. God is very close to each one of these boys. He speaks the right answer into their minds or sends other people to be of help.

God wants to help you at all times. He can come into your mind and heart. You have only to ask him, without fear, believing that he will show you the best way. But it's not easy to live without fear or have enough faith to believe that God will always hear you and answer you. How do you overcome your fear and strengthen your faith in God? By believing that God is a good God. How do you know this? Because Jesus came to show us God's love.

You are the one who will decide what you must do. Facing up to problems and solving them with God's help are a part of growing up and will help you grow as Jesus did "in wisdom and in stature, and in favor with God and man" (Luke 2:52 RSV).

Henry's Secret Plan

"We can park our bikes in that rack under the maple trees," Henry called over his shoulder as he and Carl spun up the driveway to the retirement home.

"Why do they need bicycle racks at a retirement home?" Carl asked as they chained their bikes to the metal posts.

"For the people who live here. They ride all over this property and down the back roads. I've seen them. They're a pretty lively bunch."

"You're kidding!"

"Nope. Wait till you meet my grandma. You'll see what I mean. She used to 'break' horses."

Henry and Carl bounced up the steps to the lobby and turned down a corridor leading past a row of apartment doors. Some were open, and the occupants smiled and waved as they went past. Henry stopped at a bright yellow door and knocked importantly. "Hey, Grandma, it's me, Henry."

The door flew open and a little lady with twinkly brown eyes, looking remarkably like Henry and not much taller, flung her arms around him. "What a pleasant surprise! Come in, come in, Henry. And your friend too."

Henry introduced them. "Is it true you used to break horses, Mrs. Perkins?" Carl blurted out.

"Well, I prefer to call it 'gentling," but, yes, in my day I have trained a few to saddle and bit. Lovely animals, horses. But let's not talk about the past. I'm on my way down to the craft center. Come along. I'll show you what we do there."

They entered a large, sunny room bustling with activity. In one corner two men were varnishing a small table, another was building a martin house, several people were painting at easels. Henry's grandmother led them to a table where a number of women were working with yarn. Some knitted or crocheted sweaters, and one was weaving place mats.

"Is this what you do, Grandma?" asked Henry.

"Gracious no, I'm all thumbs with yarn. But I want my friends here to meet you and Carl. Then I'll show you what my hobby is."

They chatted a few minutes with the ladies, then threaded their way to a long bench under a row of windows where a lone man worked. "Good morning, Walter. This is my grandson, Henry, and his friend, Carl. I thought I'd show them what I'm learning from you these days."

"Glad to meet you, boys," said Walter, wiping

his hands on a rag. "Your grandmother is an apt pupil. Some of her work is better than mine."

"Airplanes!" gasped both boys at once. "You build model airplanes?"

"Sure, why not?" Grandma replied. "I'm even looking forward to entering a competition meet over at Zanesville when I've had a little practice."

Henry examined a model of the space shuttle *Enterprise*. "I've always wanted to build model airplanes."

Walter smiled invitingly. "Come on out any time. Be glad to add you to the class."

Henry gazed around the room. "What do you do with all the things you make?"

"That's becoming a problem," admitted Grandma Perkins, shaking her head. "We're so productive. We really ought to have an outlet, someplace we can sell or even give away our crafts. Maybe an idea will occur to someone soon. Meanwhile, we store our creations in that closet over there. It's beginning to bulge."

After a late lunch in Grandma's apartment, Henry and Carl pedaled back to town. "I believe I'll take Walter up on his offer to help me build a plane," Henry announced. "I can take it with me to church camp next month. You and I will have a good time flying it."

Carl cleared his throat and looked at the ground. "I've been wondering how to tell you this, Henry. I guess I won't be going to camp this summer."

Henry stared at his friend dumbfounded. "Not going to camp! But we've always gone to camp together. Camp won't be any fun without you. Why aren't you going?"

"My dad says we can't spare the money right now." Carl's voice was small and tight.

"Oh!"

Henry slowly rode home after saying good-bye to Carl. He felt as if he'd just been punched in the stomach. Camp without Carl was unthinkable. Thoughts raced through Henry's head. If he took all his savings—if he asked his dad to add enough— Henry sighed. He knew Carl was too proud to accept their help. Then what? He parked his bike in the garage and went up to his room. He'd think about something happy, like building model airplanes with Walter.

On Tuesday Henry rode back to the retirement home. Tucked under one arm he carried a model airplane kit—a T33 Jet Trainer. Walter and Grandma were already busy. Henry slid into a place at the bench and opened up his kit. So many pieces! But under Walter's instruction, it began to take shape.

While waiting at one stage for the glue to dry, Henry thought again about Carl. Carl might enjoy making a model airplane. He'd bring him along next week. It would take Carl's mind off losing out on camp. Camp. A sadness welled up in Henry. He looked around the room, his eyes coming to rest on the craft-filled closet. Something clicked inside him. He sat up straight.

"Grandma, remember when you said you were looking for something to do with all your crafts?" Henry took a deep breath. "How would you like to

have a sale? A send-a-youth-to-camp sale?" He explained about Carl. "There probably are a few other kids at church who can't afford camp this summer either. Profits from your sale could pay their way. What do you say?"

Grandma Perkins' eyes crinkled up. "Sounds good to me."

"Me too," added Walter. "We'll need to talk it over with the others, of course. But I believe they'll like the idea."

Grandma adjusted the elevator on the Corsair F4U she was holding. "Do you think people will come all the way out here to buy our products?"

There was a long silence. Then, "I'll speak to Pastor Eades," said Henry. "I'll bet we can hold the sale at church. It's on a busy corner. And we can advertise." He warmed to his plan. "Some of our mothers would be glad to help transport your crafts. We kids can contribute too. We'll bring a bunch of our outgrown toys to sell."

"Fine. One thing bothers me though," said Grandma. "Won't this be embarrassing for Carl?"

"He won't ever know," declared Henry confidently. "We'll call it a church-support sale and let Pastor Eades give out the camp scholarships. The church helps people with money that is collected in many ways. Our helping Carl—and others—will be a secret among the four of us. It will be our secret plan. OK?"

Grandma and Walter nodded.

So it was that on a beautiful Saturday morning not long afterward, Henry wrestled a long table into place on the church parking lot. He whistled cheerfully. This was going to be a great success. There was still a half hour until the sale opened, and customers were already lining up. Through the crowd he glimpsed Carl approaching, his arms loaded with games and stuffed animals. Henry chuckled. "Little does he know he's helping himself," Henry murmured. "I'll not tell any of my friends. This is a secret just between you and me, God. And Grandma, Walter, and Pastor Eades, of course."

> Trust in the Lord, and do good;
> so you will dwell in the land, and
> enjoy security.
>
> Psalm 37:3 RSV

Dear God, what a feeling of peace and joy fills me when I do good in secret. Help me to understand that praise from my family and friends is not always necessary. The knowledge that you are working with me and through me is reward enough. Amen

A Matter of Trust

Kevin ran down the school steps to the wheel-chair where Barney was waiting for him.

"Any luck?" asked Barney.

"It's all set. He thinks it's a great idea." Kevin whirled Barney's chair around and around as they both cheered.

"Now to work out the details," Kevin said as he pushed Barney home. "Let's get our homework done now, and I'll be over right after dinner."

Homework and dinner done, Kevin ran across the yard to Barney's home. The two boys had been close friends for years. They had studied and played to-gether until Barney had been permanently injured in an automobile accident. Confined to a wheelchair, Barney had become withdrawn. He went only to classes, refusing to talk to or see anyone, including Kevin. This continued until two months ago when

Kevin had taken a newspaper picture to show Barney.

Kevin knew he would never forget that night. Barney had not wanted to see him, but Kevin had been asking in his prayers for some way to help his friend, trusting God to show him the way. He considered the newspaper picture an answer from God. So he went into Barney's room over his protests. "Look, Barney!" he had said. "Look at this picture of these wheelchair athletes."

"What do you mean, wheelchair athletes?"

"See—they're having races and discus throwing."

Barney had looked at the picture.

"Remember how we were training to compete in the relay races when we got to high school?" Kevin asked. "Well, you have to be fifteen years old to enter this meet and that gives you three years to train."

"You mean I should train for this competition?"

"Sure. Why not?" Kevin replied. "I'll be your manager. Of course you'll need one." Both boys had laughed at that. It was the first time in months Barney had laughed. Now, weeks later, they were making new plans.

"How come the principal agreed?" asked Barney.

"I took the coach in with me, and he helped persuade Mr. Cornwall. Seems the coach had been watching us practice mornings. He came early to school one morning and saw you pumping like mad down the tennis court. Guess he thought you'd gone crazy until he heard me yell, 'You cut three seconds off your best time.' He's seen us several times since then and was a pushover for our idea.

"What we have to do tonight is to write out the

information for a flyer so it can be included in the invitations to the spring track meet of the Tri-Valley Schools."

They worked on the project together and, after scratching and rewriting the message several times, both Kevin and Barney were pleased with the final result. Barney read out loud:

If you are disabled and/or in a wheelchair, you are invited to participate in a mini-meet to precede the annual track meet.
Wheelchair races will be run on the tennis courts, discus throwing nearby. This is the first of what will be an annual event!
Please fill in the attached registration form and send with registrations for the other events. . . .

"I wish we had something a team could do together, like we used to. If it wasn't for you, I wouldn't be in this."

Both boys were silent, trying to think of some event they could do together.

"I wonder—" said Kevin.

"You wonder what?"

"Could you pitch horseshoes?" asked Kevin.

"Horseshoes! Where'd you get that idea?"

"We always play horseshoes when we go to Grandpa's farm."

"How do you play?"

"There are two short stakes in the ground some distance apart. You pitch a horseshoe to make it land over the stake. That's called a 'ringer.' You get points for a 'leaner' and distances from the stake. Team members stand at opposite ends and pitch against the opposing member of the other team. We could have one person in a wheelchair and a stand-up partner at either end. That way the horseshoes could be picked up, scores kept, and so on. It's a natural! What do you think?"

"Where would we get the stakes and horseshoes?" asked Barney.

"Grandpa'd be right here with all we need."

"It sounds great. Let's add it to the flyer." So they wrote:

P.S. Wheelchair competitors with a stand-up partner are urged to compete in a horseshoe-throwing contest. It doesn't matter if you don't know what it is or have never played the game. We guarantee FUN!!

The next morning, Kevin and Barney took their message to Mr. Cornwall. The principal's office was a busy place, but Mr. Cornwall called the boys into his private office. "Let's see what you have," he said. "Very good. *Very good.* This is a wonderful idea. Whose was it?"

"Kevin's," said Barney.

"We worked it out together," Kevin said.

"No matter. We're all looking forward to it."

Now Barney and Kevin worked out in earnest. Barney continued to roll faster over the course they had laid out. He kept throwing the discus a little farther each day. Grandpa was bringing the stakes and horseshoes himself and asked if he could referee the matches.

Everything was ready. But would there be any

entries for the mini-meet? None came in the first week, and gloom descended on the boys.

"Take it easy," said the coach. "This is brand-new. People have to think about it. There's going to be a meeting of all the coaches for the track meet. I'll talk it up there."

One reservation came in. Then three. By the deadline, there were ten contestants for the wheelchair race, seven for the discus throw and eight teams for the horseshoe throw.

The entire school became interested. The cheerleaders practiced new cheers for the mini-meet, and the band members said they'd march them in.

On the big day, parents and students crowded around the tennis court to watch the wheelchair race, ran out of the way of the discus throwers, and joined in the fun at the horseshoe meet.

Barney rolled in first in the wheelchair race, to the cheers of his friends. He was third in the discus throw. No one seemed to know who won the horseshoe-throwing contests because everyone laughed so much. Grandpa declared every team a winner and gave them all horseshoe badges.

That night after it was all over and Barney and Kevin were together, Barney said, "What a day it was! How can we ever thank you, Kevin, me especially! I bet I'd still be sitting by myself in that old wheelchair if it wasn't for you."

"Don't thank me, Barney. We all worked together. But you know, God was behind it all—like I told you that first night when I brought the picture over."

Commit your way to the Lord;
trust in him, and he will act.
Psalm 37:5 RSV

Help me to always remember you are there, God, willing and wanting to help me. May I trust you at all times and recognize and follow your leading. Amen

A Spoonful of Courage

Turning the gray mare away from the lake, Scott trotted slowly up to the gate of the adjoining fenced-in field. He loved these early morning rides along the edge of the lake, the horse's feet splashing with a rhythmic beat as they cantered in the shallow water. Misty, too, seemed to enjoy them, tossing her head in the sweet air, pricking her ears to catch familiar sounds.

Now came the hard part. Scott's legs tightened as he entered the gate. Misty, alert to his tension, danced nervously. "Come on, Misty," he crooned, patting her neck. "Jump for me this time. Please!" He cantered in a large circle, then moved the horse down center field toward the white poles of a hurdle set up in the middle. The closer they got, the higher the poles loomed. Scott's hands trembled on the reins. He shut his eyes. Misty, sensing no control from her master, instead of gathering herself to jump, halted abruptly at the hurdle. Scott slid unceremoniously over her neck to sprawl on the grass on the opposite side of the poles. Dusting himself off, he heaved a big sigh. He had failed again.

This month at church camp had started out like Christmas every day for Scott. Each boy was given a horse to care for and learn with. An immediate love affair sprang up between Scott and Misty. She responded quickly and willingly to his commands, and Scott appreciated her intelligence and gentleness. Jim, the riding instructor, told him Misty was part Arabian. It showed in her dappled gray coat, in the way she carried her tail high, and in her affection for people.

Scott and Misty spent hours together, exploring the woods or playing in the lake. Misty liked to swim almost as much as Scott did. He would float beside her, grasping her mane in his hands, guiding her by pressure on her shoulders.

Only one problem marred the days. So far, Scott had not been able to persuade Misty to jump over the hurdles. And that was a requirement if he expected to participate in the gymkhana at the end of this week. The gymkhana was the highlight of the camping session, with everyone engaging in games on horseback. There would be barrel races, obstacle courses, and, of course, jumping competition. What was he going to do?

Gathering up the reins, Scott led Misty back to the barn. "We'll try again after lunch, Misty," he said as he removed her saddle and bridle. He ran a brush over her back where the saddle had lain, then turned her into her stall. After checking to make sure plenty of water and hay were available, Scott dashed off to his own lunch.

The dining hall pulsed with its usual uproar of clattering dishes punctuated by the laughter and shouting of boys. Scott filled his tray. Farther back in line, Howie from Scott's church leaned forward with a mischievous grin. "Hey, Scott," he yelled loud enough for all to hear, "you got that mare of yours over the jumps yet? You're running out of time."

Scott felt his face turn red. "Don't you worry, I'll make it," he threw back and stomped determinedly to sit with Jim. He wouldn't let the rest know how much it hurt. "Jim," he said in a low voice, "when you ride Misty, she behaves perfectly. But she refuses to jump for me. She follows all my other directions. What am I doing wrong?" he pleaded.

Jim laid down his fork. "She doesn't trust you completely yet, Scott. I've been watching you. When you approach the hurdles, you're not sure of yourself. Your insecurity transfers to Misty. When you're not at ease, she gets nervous too. Then she runs out to one side of the hurdle or stops. When you gain confidence in yourself, then she'll settle down and skim over the jumps. Keep working. Basically you're a good horseman." Jim squeezed Scott's shoulder and left.

Scott stirred his pudding into a runny mess. "What he's really saying is that I'm scared," thought Scott. "And it's true." He blinked hard to keep tears from starting.

With sagging shoulders he walked back to the barn. Misty heard his step and nickered softly. "I'll work into it easy," Scott decided as he saddled Misty and rode back to the field. Courses for the gymkhana were already laid out so the boys could practice. Scott ran through the barrel race course, noting with pride how gracefully Misty shifted her weight on the sharp turns. Next he led her over the make-believe bridge, opening and closing the gate beyond. Misty didn't shy once. His spirits lifting, Scott circled at the far end of the field and showed Misty the jump in center field. "C'mon, girl. This time, huh?" he murmured, increasing speed. But as they neared the jump, Scott knew Misty was going to run out to one side. She did.

Shrill laughter rang out. Looking up, Scott spotted Howie in the middle of the lake. He was paddling a kayak. Scott recognized it as one Howie and another boy had been building in craft class. "Chicken!" shouted Howie.

"Never mind that," Scott answered stiffly. "What are you doing out in the lake by yourself? That's against rules."

"Aw, who's to know? Besides, I can handle myself better than some other people can." And he laughed again.

Scorning him, Scott turned away to try the barrel course again. Misty performed smoothly. They were just leaving the last barrel when a cry for help brought Scott's head up sharply. Checking Misty, he glanced around. Frantic thrashing in the middle of the lake caught his eye, and he froze. One end of Howie's kayak pointed skyward, the other dipped underneath the water. And struggling to escape from the well was Howie.

"Help! Help me, Scott," called Howie, panic in his voice. "I'm caught. The kayak is pulling apart at the seams. It's sinking. Do something!" He flailed his arms, trying to keep the light craft afloat by beating the water.

Scott's heart stood still. Howie was in danger of drowning. What could he do? Even as he considered galloping out the gate and around the fence to the lake, he realized he would be too late. There was no way he could rescue Howie, unless. . . . An idea so fantastic hit Scott that he swayed in the saddle. Could he do it?

With icy fingers, he picked up the reins and took Misty to the center of the ring. Then, pointing her head toward the fence that separated them from the lake front, he signaled her to canter. Straight toward the fence they charged. Scott's mouth filled with dust, his heart pounded louder than Misty's feet. In his mind he could hear Jim's advice: Maintain light contact with your horse's mouth. Let her pace herself. Don't interfere with her way of going as you approach the poles. Loosen the reins as she takes off. Grip the saddle with your knees. Keep your heels down! All of a sudden Scott's fear fell away. He was no longer afraid.

The fence still rushed at him, appearing to grow in size. That no longer bothered Scott. But Misty faltered. "Don't fail me. Go, Misty, go!" Scott spoke firmly, touching the mare with his heels. Responding, Misty tucked up her legs and soared over the fence. Without slowing, they ran into the water and started swimming. Scott slipped from Misty's back and

shoved her toward Howie whose chin now rested on the water. "Hang on, Howie, we're coming!"

Seconds later, Scott freed Howie from the broken kayak, and they started back to shore. "Grab hold of Misty's tail," he ordered Howie. "Let her pull you."

Once on the shore, Scott and Howie shook water out of their hair, laughing as Misty did the same. "Thank you, Scott," said Howie, growing serious. "I'll never tease you again. That was the most beautiful jump I've ever seen. A four-foot fence, and you sailed over it like a Frisbee. Jumping like that might win you high points at the gymkhana Friday."

Scott grinned and poked Howie in the ribs. "That wouldn't surprise me at all." Then as Misty rubbed her head up and down his wet jersey, he laughed again.

> Be strong and of good courage; be not frightened, neither be dismayed; for the Lord your God is with you wherever you go.
> Joshua 1:9 RSV

Dear God, show me how to be strong and courageous. Help me to believe that you are always beside me, guiding me, instructing me, loving me. Increase my faith, so that I know you are close even when I don't sense your presence. Amen

The New Door

Paul's mother came into his bedroom. "The doctor just telephoned, Paul. The tests have come in."

"There's nothing the matter with me, is there, Mother? I can get up, can't I?"

"I'm afraid not, dear. You see, the doctor says you have rheumatic fever."

"What's rheumatic fever?"

"A fever caused by a low-grade infection. Along with medicine, the only cure is complete quiet and rest. You must remain flat in bed for two weeks, and then have bed rest for two or three more weeks."

Paul sat up abruptly. "Stay in bed for a month! I'll lose my place on the baseball team and miss camp! And what about school?"

"You can do some schoolwork later on. I know it's going to be hard, but if you rest now, the doctor says your heart will not be permanently damaged. You will be able to play baseball again—probably next year."

"Next year? I want to do it now!" Paul turned to the wall. He wouldn't cry! But this was worse than anything he had imagined. "Can my friends come to see me? Is it catching?"

"No, it's not catching, and your friends can come later to see you. For awhile, though, you can have no company. I'll get your medicine and a milk shake now, Paul. You just rest."

That evening Paul's father came to his bedside. "We're sorry, son. But it's wonderful to know that if you rest you will be well and strong again. We'll do all we can to help you. You're facing a different kind of test than winning a place on the baseball team. You will be fighting a different kind of fight, but one you can win with God's help."

It wasn't fair! Paul knew he would lose his place on the team. Yet he had to admit to himself it was good to be able to lie still and do nothing now that he didn't have to worry about baseball, or the team, or school. He went to sleep.

He began to feel better. He could sit up, dangle his legs over the side of the bed, watch his favorite TV shows. But he did get tired of doing nothing all the time.

"Mom, I've got to *do* something. I'm going crazy. Why can't I get up?"

"You've done so well, Paul, you don't want to do anything now that will spoil it. Miss Sullivan stopped by while you were asleep. She brought the new history book your class is studying. She thinks you will enjoy reading it."

"I'm tired of reading. I want to *do* something," Paul grumbled.

"When you say your prayers, Paul, have you asked God for help? He can open a new door for you."

"Open a door? What do you mean?"

"Think of a door as a new opportunity."

Paul prayed that night for a new door. The next day he tried to think of a new opportunity to do something. Then he remembered the model airplane kit he had received for Christmas. Too busy with baseball, he had done nothing with it.

His mother was happy to bring the kit, the glue, and the necessary tools, with a big board on which Paul could work in bed. He cut and glued until dinner time. The next day he worked, stopping only for naps when his mother reminded him. When his father came home, Paul showed him the finished airplane.

"Hey, son, that's great," his father said. "Let's see how well it flies."

He gave the plane a sharp push upwards, and it soared to the ceiling. "Wait till we take it outdoors. It's a great flyer."

Well, that's that, thought Paul. But what next?

He picked up the book Miss Sullivan had brought, *The History of Transportation.* As Paul read, a new door opened. The Bright Idea, he called it. He talked it over with Mother and Father and they agreed it was indeed a bright idea.

33

"A great idea," said Father. "A new door!" said Mother.

The next evening, Paul's father came home with several packages. Paul opened them and thought he couldn't wait until morning to begin his new work.

The days passed quickly now. Mother would have to say, "Time to rest a bit, Paul. You must not undo all the progress you've made."

Friends could come to visit for short periods. They told Paul of their preparations for the upcoming school Science Fair. "I'm going to have an exhibit too," Paul told them. They begged to know what he was doing, but he kept his project a secret.

Paul's health continued to improve. He could walk around his bedroom, then go downstairs, and, finally, walk in the yard. Mother made a chocolate cake to celebrate.

"My exhibit is all done, Father," Paul said one night. "Do you think it's all right?"

"Indeed I do," he said. "You've done very fine work, and it will be of interest to everyone."

Mother bought red poster board and Paul made a big, bright sign for his exhibit.

The doctor said, "Yes, Paul may go to the Science Fair. In fact, I'm going too. I want to see what my special patient has been up to."

When the night of the Science Fair came, Father, Mother, and Paul had many boxes to carry—boxes which they handled very carefully.

Miss Sullivan met them at the door of the school. "We're all so glad you could come, Paul," she said. "I've saved this table for your exhibit. Is it large enough?"

34

"Yes, thank you. It's really good to be back in the school again," Paul said. Everyone smiled.

Then Paul set up his exhibit. He took from the boxes many types of small wooden engines. One had a very tall smokestack, one had a firebox, another a cowcatcher, and one a bell that could be rung. Some of the engines were pulling passenger cars with open windows. Others pulled flat cars, one of which was carrying little wooden barrels. Above the models on the table he put his sign: *History of the Steam Engine.*

Paul's friends clustered around him. "It's good to see you. Are you coming back to school now?" The baseball coach said, "I'll expect you back next year."

The program began with a welcoming speech and the school song. Then Miss Sullivan said, "Before we go into the exhibit room, I would like Paul to explain his project to us."

Paul stood up. "While I was sick, I read in our history book about transportation. I decided to make models of the different kinds of engines. Thanks to my Dad and Mom, who did all the running, I was able to do this. Now you can see what trains looked like when they had steam engines."

Everyone clapped. Then Miss Sullivan spoke again. "Paul is giving his model collection to the class. That way other students may also see how engines have changed. Thank you, Paul. Your exhibit will be enjoyed by many."

This time the clapping was louder than before. Paul turned to his mother after thanking everyone. "God did open a new door, didn't he?"

"And you walked right through it," she answered.

So then, as often as we have the chance, we should do good to everyone.

Galatians 6:10 TEV

Dear God, help me to keep from being discouraged, to see new opportunities in what seems like failure or defeat. Help me discover "new doors" in my life. In Jesus' name. Amen

Ricky's Private Work Camp

Ricky hopped on his bike and rode away from church, glancing nervously at the sky. The sun had already disappeared. "It's later than I imagined," he told himself. "Mom will be anxious. Staying after fellowship was not such a good idea." But he and his friends were so excited about their work-camp trip to Edmington there had been lots to talk about.

Coming to a corner, Ricky decided to take a shortcut through an unfamiliar alley to save time. He pedaled along mechanically, dodging trash cans and weeds, his mind on Tuesday coming up. The group would go by bus to the church camp just outside Edmington where they would sleep and eat, with plenty of time for swimming, hiking, and games. But each day they would also spend some time cleaning, painting, and making repairs for a number of people in town who needed their help. Ricky felt grown-up and useful. Not many kids his age had a chance like this. Not even his older brother, Chris, had been on a work-camp outing.

As he braked before turning into his own street, Ricky's eyes skimmed over the yard beside him. "What a mess," he mumbled, taking in the rickety fence, the sagging gate, the ground peppered with soft-drink containers and last fall's leaves. "That place looks like Disasterville."

He sped up his street, forgetting about the messy yard and all else as he approached his own house. Lights blazed from every window, and his little sister sat on the front steps—crying.

"Oh, Ricky," she burst out as he zoomed up the driveway, "something awful has happened. Chris fell off his bike and broke his ankle. He's at the hospital with Mom and Dad. And he's worried. Miss Johnson from next door is in the house, but Chris made me promise to wait right here and ask you—will you deliver his papers for him until his ankle is well?"

Ricky knew it would be several weeks before Chris could deliver papers again. Of course he would be glad to carry Chris's papers, except for—Ricky's heart dived down to his toes—for this week! What would he do about this week? He couldn't give up his trip, he wouldn't. His mind raced over the possibilities. Maybe Mom—or Dad. . . . Even as he thought, he rejected the idea. There was hardly time enough now for all his parents had to do. And his friends who weren't going on the trip with him were vacationing. "Sure," he said weakly, forcing a smile to his face. "Come in the house, Susie."

Long after Mom and Dad and Chris returned home, with Chris cuddled and fussed over in bed, Ricky lay awake. "What am I going to do, God?" he prayed. "Going to Edmington means working for you. I've got to go. Please find someone to carry Chris's papers this week." Feeling better, he drifted off to sleep, confident that in the morning God would answer his prayer.

But in the early morning light, as he dropped newspapers on porches and steps, no answer came. "Please hurry, God," Ricky whispered. "There isn't much time left."

Ricky tightened his mouth. "Why did Chris have to break his ankle right now? Why, why, why?" he demanded, picking up a stick and beating it against a fence he was passing. With each "why" he beat harder. To his dismay, several boards in the fence crashed to the ground. Ricky recognized the fence. It was the one he had noticed yesterday—at the disaster place. Should he go up to the door of the house and tell the owner about the damage he had done? He could see lights in what seemed to be a kitchen. Why bother? Everything about the place was so run down the owner probably wouldn't see the broken boards. He would just leave and say nothing. But something inside nagged at him. Was that the way a responsible Christian behaved? Slowly Ricky walked up the path and knocked timidly on a weather-beaten door. The name *Gardner* was etched above the brass knocker.

The door creaked open, and Ricky found himself staring at a frail little lady with a tired smile. "Yes?" she inquired. "What is it?"

Ricky gulped and told her.

When he had finished, the lady gazed at him with sad eyes. "What a nice young man you are," she said. "Not like those others who throw trash in my yard. My arthritis is so bad it keeps me from cleaning up properly. I know it looks unkempt. I guess that's why other people treat my property as a dumping place."

"Well, uh, ah—," Ricky stammered, "I'll be glad to come back this afternoon and nail up the boards I knocked down."

"Would you?" Miss Gardner smiled her tired smile. "That's very kind of you."

Right after lunch Ricky brought some tools and began hammering the boards back into place. As he worked, he again asked God to find someone to carry Chris's papers so he could go on the work-camp trip. But he didn't have much hope now. The rest of the group would be leaving in the morning, and he, Ricky, would have to stay home. He didn't mind so much missing the games and hiking. At Camp Pine Hollow later in the summer he would have his fill of fun things. No, what Ricky wanted to do was to show his Christian concern, to show himself a good neighbor. "I suppose God doesn't think my problem's important enough. He's not going to do anything to help me." Ricky sighed.

He finished the boards. "As long as I'm here, I might as well mend the hinges on that gate," Ricky murmured to himself. When he had fixed the hinges, he had another idea. He went to Miss Gardner's garage and got out a rake and some trash sacks. He

began to whistle as he vigorously attacked the leaves and debris in the yard.

As the trash sacks filled up, Ricky leaned on his rake and examined the house. "That porch could sure use a coat of paint. I'll ask Miss Gardner if she'd like me to paint it for her some afternoon. And while she's deciding on that, I can be washing the windows."

Suddenly Ricky drew in his breath sharply. "This is exactly the kind of work my friends in fellowship will be doing at Edmington," he thought in amazement. "I've got my own private work-camp right here. I don't need to go away to be a good neighbor. There are lots of things I can do to help Miss Gardner. Is that what you've been telling me, God, that I am needed more here than at Edmington?" Deep inside, Ricky knew it was true. "I was so wrapped up in my disappointment, I forgot that you always provide the best answer to a problem. After this, my trust will be stronger."

Ricky flourished the rake once more and whistled up a storm, planning all the things he would do to help Miss Gardner—with her permission, of course.

> Wait for the Lord; be strong,
> and let your heart take courage;
> yea, wait for the Lord!
> Psalm 27:14 RSV

Dear God, teach me patience. Help me to be calm, to know that you will lead me to the right decision at the right time. Amen

Seventy Times Seven

From his seat high in his favorite tree, Chuck saw his sister Susie come out of the house and head for her hideaway in the far corner of the front yard. She was carrying a large green and white box.

"Susie!" Chuck yelled. "Take that box back. That's mine!" Chuck began climbing down the tree as fast as he could.

Susie, who was younger than Chuck by three years, had been told many times not to play with Chuck's things. The green and white box had been a birthday gift from Uncle Dan. It contained a collection of sample rocks with their names and characteristics to help Chuck identify them, for Chuck wanted to be a geologist. Susie had looked at the rocks with Chuck and had been told this was very special and only Chuck would handle the box and its contents. Chuck had kept the box on top of his bookcase. Susie must have climbed on a chair to get it down.

Jumping from the lowest branch, Chuck ran to the front yard, only to be met by a Susie in tears. "Oh, Chuck," she wailed. "I didn't mean to, but I slipped and your rocks spilled all over the ground. I'm sorry —I didn't mean—" and Susie cried harder than ever.

"You had no business taking them in the first place," Chuck shouted. "You were told to stay out of my room and never to touch that box. You had no right to take it!"

"I just wanted to look at the pretty rocks. I'll help —" Susie cried, hanging onto Chuck's arm.

"Let go of me! Get out of my way! Go away!" Chuck yelled.

Mother heard the commotion and came into the yard. "What's all the trouble?" she asked.

"Susie took my geology box and spilled all the rocks. Now I'll never find them," Chuck cried.

"I'm sorry," Susie sobbed. "I didn't mean to spill them. I'll help find them. I'm a good looker."

"We'll both help you find the rocks," Mother said. "Then we'll talk about Susie taking them."

"I don't want any help," shouted Chuck, and he ran to the place where the green and white box lay upside down on the grass.

"Very well, Chuck. Come, Susie, we'll go into the house and straighten this out later."

Left alone, Chuck, on his hands and knees, searched in the grass for his rocks. The larger ones were easy to find, but he knew he did not find all the smaller stones.

Chuck had been so surprised and happy with this

gift. He had been studying so he could recognize different kinds of rocks and how to identify them. Now he would never know. He would *never* forgive Susie. Picking up his box, he went to his room, slammed the door, and stayed there until called for dinner.

Only Mother, Susie, and Chuck were at the dinner table that night. Chuck's father was away on business. The meal was an unhappy one. Chuck refused to talk or eat. Susie's eyes were red and tears came easily.

Mother had said, "We will talk about this afternoon's trouble after dinner. Mealtime should be pleasant." But as Chuck remained silent and did not eat the food on his plate, she said, "Chuck, if you do not care to eat or talk, we will excuse you. You are being rude."

Chuck got up from the table and slammed out of the house. It was too dark to climb his tree. He sat down with his back against the trunk, hunched against the wind.

"Now I'm blamed for being rude and sent from the table. It's all Susie's fault. It isn't fair! If only Dad were here, he'd understand," thought Chuck. Dad would sympathize with his anger. But would he? Suddenly Chuck remembered another time when he had been angry at his best friend.

"Being angry never solves anything," Dad had said. "What you must do is discover why you are angry. Then think how the problem that makes you angry can be solved. Only when you have done something to resolve the problem will you be at peace with yourself."

"I'm certainly not at peace with myself now," thought Chuck. He had felt so good that afternoon up in his tree. Now his head ached. His heart ached too when he thought of Susie's tearful face, of Mother and her disappointment at his behavior. "But Susie had no right—" Chuck checked his thoughts. "I must not get angry again," he told himself.

How many rocks had he lost? Probably not too many, and he and Susie could look again tomorrow. He and Susie? He had told her he didn't want her help, and now he was including her in tomorrow's search. Even though she was younger and a girl, they did have fun together. How angry and unkind he had been.

Suddenly Chuck knew he must see Susie. He ran to the house. Mother was sitting on the porch. He slowed to a walk and went up the steps.

"I'm sorry I was so rude at dinner," he said.

"You were angry, Chuck, and when we are angry we do unkind things."

"I know. And . . . I'm sorry about Susie. Even if it was her fault, getting angry didn't help. How can I make things right?"

"Susie showed you the way."

"She did? How?" asked Chuck.

"She said she was sorry and offered to help find the rocks, trying to repair the trouble she had caused."

"And I didn't listen. Do you suppose she's asleep yet? May I find out?"

Mother nodded and Chuck went up the stairs as quietly as he could. By the hall light he saw Susie sitting up in her bed with the blankets bundled around her. "Susie?" he whispered.

"Oh, Chuck! I was hoping you'd come. I'm so sorry," and she began to cry.

Chuck climbed onto the bed and put his arms around his sister. "Susie, please don't cry anymore. I'm sorry I was so angry."

"You're not mad now?"

"No."

"I'm so glad. And I won't take anything of yours any more. Mother said I was very naughty."

"Well, I wasn't much better myself," Chuck laughed. "Tomorrow morning we'll look for the rocks I couldn't find."

"You mean I can help you?"

"Yes, Susie, I need your help."

"Oh, Chuck, you're the nicest brother," she said, and with a contented sigh, Susie lay down and was instantly asleep.

Chuck came downstairs to sit on the porch steps.

"Was she awake, Chuck?"

"Yes, I think she was waiting for me. Tomorrow we're both going to look for the missing rocks." With a sigh Chuck said, "I guess I can sleep now that everything is right between us."

"The apostle Paul understood that feeling," Mother said. "He wrote to the people in Ephesus, 'Do not let the sun go down on your anger' (4:26). Now, Chuck, how about a piece of pie before going to bed?" And they went into the kitchen.

> Then Peter came up and said to him, "Lord, how often shall my brother sin against me, and I forgive him? As many as seven

47

times?" Jesus said to him, "I do not say to you seven times, but seventy times seven."

Matthew 18:21-22 RSV

Dear God, please keep me from anger. But if I do become angry, help me learn to forgive those people I think have injured me and to work with them to set everything right again. In Jesus' name. Amen

Bike Ride to Friendship

Paul took a deep breath and let his fingers drop lightly to the keyboard. Out of the corner of his eye he saw Eric, sitting in a front pew, smirk and poke the boy next to him. Paul knew the smirk was meant for him, and it hurt. But pushing the feeling to the back of his mind, he turned all his attention to the Beethoven piano sonata he was playing. Paul was proud to have been asked to play the prelude music at Sunday morning worship, and he wanted to play his very best.

Later, though, as he rode home on his bike, the hurt again welled up in him. This town was going to be no different from all the others. Paul's dad transferred often in his job, necessitating frequent moves for the family. When he was little, Paul didn't mind. But as he grew older, he changed. This last move had been the hardest. His new classmates at school and church formed a tight little circle, excluding him. They weren't interested in him or his ideas. Like the time he suggested that his church fellowship group take a course in cardiopulmonary resuscitation—CPR. Stony silence had greeted his proposal. After that Paul quit trying and stayed on the fringes, turning more and more to his first love, music.

Absorbed in his thoughts, it was several minutes before he heard someone hailing him. "Hey, Paul, wait up. I want to ask you something."

Paul looked back. Eric and Jeffrey, another member of the youth fellowship, were pedaling toward him. Eric ran his fingers through his hair in an embarrassed manner as he skidded to a halt. "Uh—you know about the bike race coming up, don't you?" he asked.

Paul nodded. Youth Fellowship had buzzed with nothing else ever since St. Luke's Fellowship had challenged them to a time trial bike race. The losing side would treat the winners to a hayride and wiener roast.

"Well," continued Eric, "we need one more guy for our team. Will you help us out?"

Pleasure, then despair, surged through Paul as he realized he was a last-minute choice. He tightened his jaw, remembering Eric's gesture in church. Let them be short a team member. He didn't care. "Sorry, I have to practice," he flung out.

"Can't you take some time off?" demanded Eric, blocking Paul's bike. "Do you spend all your free hours practicing?"

Paul drew himself up. "If I want to be a career pianist, I must work hard. That means sacrificing and giving up other activities. I'll bet Van Cliburn didn't waste his energies time-trialing when he was my age."

Eric appeared taken aback at the vehemence in Paul's voice. "Will you at least think it over? We're making a practice spin Saturday morning. If you change your mind, meet us at church about nine o'clock. Bring a sandwich. We plan to stay out until around three."

As he and Jeffrey rode off, Eric's words floated back to Paul. "Beats me why a guy wants to bury his nose in a bunch of music all the time. Most of it sounds like sour notes to me."

"I think he's pretty good myself," responded Jeffrey, "and during the season you're every bit as wrapped up in baseball."

"Maybe."

Paul went on home. He wouldn't go, he wouldn't. But Saturday morning while he stood brushing his teeth, he wavered. Probably the others thought he couldn't stand up to a grueling run, especially Eric who'd like nothing better than to make fun of him again. He could give Eric a surprise. Since he had few friends, Paul rode his bike a lot, and his muscles were strong and tough. "I can take hills better than any of the rest of them." Paul stuck out his tongue at his reflection in the bathroom mirror and went down to breakfast.

"Glad you could make it," Eric called out as Paul wheeled into the church parking lot.

Ignoring him, Paul headed toward Jeffrey who stood with two other boys, studying a map.

"Let's go," announced Eric, buckling on his hel-

met. The others did the same. "Let's run this like a regular competition. If one of us has a flat or has to drop out for any reason, the others keep going. It's up to the straggler to catch up. OK?"

There was a chorus of "OKs." The boys mounted and rode single file out of the parking lot and along the suburban streets. Soon they were cruising smoothly down a back road that meandered through a valley. Paul stayed behind Jeffrey. There wasn't much conversation, each boy intent on "drafting"—staying about a foot behind the rider in front of him. Paul rode confidently, maintaining a steady cadence. Grudgingly he admitted to himself that Eric made a good leader. He was pacing them well.

Before long the road climbed up out of the valley in a series of twisting hills. Now the going became difficult and the sun hot. Paul's legs began to ache, his throat rasped, perspiration trickled down his face. He noticed Jeffrey had unbuckled the strap of his helmet. They rose over the crest of a hill. The road here was narrow, the ground dropping away sharply on each side. Shifting gears, the riders plunged straight down into another valley, faster and faster. Jeffrey spread out his arms so the rush of air could dry his soaked T-shirt.

A second later, before Paul's horrified eyes, Jeffrey's bike slammed against a rut in the road. Jeffrey grabbed for the handlebars too late. Fishtailing into the air like a bucking horse, the bike swerved crazily and crashed to the pavement. Jeffrey, thrown clear, tumbled head over heels down the steep, rock-encrusted embankment, his helmet bouncing after him.

Frantically the others braked and slipped and slid their way down to the place where Jeffrey lay without moving.

Eric placed a hand on Jeffrey's chest as the others crowded around. "His head must have hit 10 rocks on the way down. He isn't breathing! What shall we do?"

"Not breathing!" Paul's voice sounded unnaturally loud in the stillness. He knew that without immediate help, Jeffrey would die. Pushing the others aside, he knelt in the dirt beside Jeffrey. His own heart pounded. Tilting Jeffrey's neck up and back, Paul pinched the boy's nostrils closed. Then, forming a suction between his mouth and Jeffrey's, he breathed quickly four times into Jeffrey's lungs. Next he slid his finger down to the carotid artery in Jeffrey's neck. He couldn't feel any pulse. "Does anyone else know how to give CPR?" he asked hopefully. No one answered.

It was up to him. Paul placed one trembling hand over the other on Jeffrey's chest, pushing sharply just below the sternum, the point where ribs and breastbone meet. "Oh, let me remember how, God," he prayed. In rapid succession he pushed 15 times, then, making a seal again over Jeffrey's mouth, he breathed twice. Then back to his chest for 15 pushes. He established a rhythmic pattern—15 pushes, then two puffs of air into Jeffrey's lungs.

He paid no attention to the other boys who stared as if mesmerized. Then Eric snapped back to reality. "You two ride down the road to a telephone. Call an ambulance," he directed.

"Right." The two scrambled up the hill and raced out of sight.

"Is there anything I can do?" asked Eric as he crouched beside Paul. "Your suggestion to Fellowship sounded so far out. I wish we had listened."

Paul didn't answer. He couldn't. He needed all his energy for his task. Hours seemed to pass. He was growing tired. How much longer could he keep this up? His head began to swim. What if he fainted? Why didn't the ambulance come? What if it didn't come at all? Paul sobbed under his breath. Then, miraculously, Jeffrey gulped and started breathing on his own. Although unconscious, his color returned. Paul let his arms drop. His shoulders slumped with fatigue.

"You saved his life," whispered Eric, a look of wonder and awe on his face. "Who would expect a guy who's glued to a piano to save someone's life? How does it feel?"

Paul spat out, "Just because I like piano doesn't mean I can't do anything else." Then, as Eric continued to gaze at him as if he were Superman, Paul grinned. "It feels great!"

Eric laughed and pounded him on the back. "You're quite a guy, Paul."

At this point, Jeffrey stirred and opened his eyes. "What happened?" he gasped.

Paul squeezed his hand. "Lie still. You had an accident, but everything's going to be all right. I hear sirens. That must be the ambulance on its way with help."

Paul and Eric followed the stretcher up the hill to the road. Eric laid his hand on Paul's arm. "Paul,

I'm sorry I made fun of your music. Can we start over again and be friends?"

"I'd like that," said Paul. He flicked an imaginary something off his shoulder. "And I'm knocking that chip off my shoulder for good. I can't expect people to accept me unless I give them a chance, can I?"

> Why do you see the speck that is in your brother's eye, but do not notice the log that is in your own eye?
>
> Matthew 7:3 RSV

Dear God, keep me from being critical of others. When they don't behave as I think they should, let me see you in them and know that we are both your children. Let this be a bond between us. Amen

Doug Keeps a Promise

Doug's thoughts were not on his buzzing lawn mower as he pushed it around Mrs. Hughes' yard. They were with his friends now on their way to the new park. In each one's bike basket was a big lunch and a pair of swim trunks. He had wanted to go with them, but he had promised Mrs. Hughes he would help her.

"Why can't I work for her on Sunday? Or after school?" he had asked at the dinner table. "Why this Saturday?"

There had been no answer from his mother or father. Nothing was said about keeping a promise, about being trusted to do what you said you'd do. Actually, nothing needed to be said. This had often been talked of after one of Doug's father's employees had failed him. There'd even been a Sunday school lesson about Peter's promising never to deny his

Lord and then going right out and doing it. The answer to Doug's question had been left to him.

Doug had struggled with the idea of telling Mrs. Hughes about the bike hike and seeing if there was another day when he could help her. But in talking with himself, he had to admit there would be other bike hikes, and her grass wouldn't wait. So here he was. A nice Saturday wasted because after he finished cutting the grass he had two flower beds to weed.

Mrs. Hughes came to the porch and beckoned to Doug. He heard her call after he switched off the mower. "You must be hot," she said. "Come join me for a few minutes." When Doug came up the front steps, she handed him a glass of cold milk and a plate of brownies. "My grandsons are dropping in today, Doug," she said. "I mean literally dropping in, because they are balloonists."

"You mean they really go up in balloons?" asked Doug.

"Yes. They're on their way to a balloon meet and race in Iowa. They said they'd drop in to see me." She laughed. "I'd like you to meet Bruce and Lester."

"I'd like to see their balloon," thought Doug. He thanked Mrs. Hughes for the milk and brownies and, feeling much better, soon finished the lawn. He was on his hands and knees weeding the front flower bed when a car stopped in front. Two young men jumped out, ran up the walk, and through the front door calling, "Gran, we're here!"

"The grandsons have dropped in," thought Doug.

The front bed was clear of weeds, so Doug moved to the border along the house. He hoped he wasn't pulling out flowers, but he recognized leaves he had seen his mother yank out of her flower beds, especially the trailing vines that overpowered everything. There! The last weed out! Doug sat on his heels and looked over his work. There was certainly an improvement, something to show for his grubby knees and hands. After putting away the tools and trash bags in the rear shed, Doug rang the front door bell.

"Hi, Doug!" one of the grandsons said. "Come on in."

"Thank you, but I just wanted to tell Mrs. Hughes I was through. I think she should check to see if everything is all right," Doug said.

"Hey, Gran, Doug wants you," the grandson called.

Mrs. Hughes came to the door and down the porch steps. Slowly she walked around the flower beds and inspected the border and lawn. She turned to Doug with a bright smile. "It's wonderful, Doug. I couldn't have done better myself. I know there must have been other things you'd rather have done on a sunny Saturday, but I thank you so very much for helping me. I'm glad to know a boy I can trust to follow through on his promises!

"Now I think I have a treat for you. How would you like a balloon ride?"

"Wow! You mean go up in a balloon with your grandsons?"

"Yes. They're leaving now but want to give you a short ride. I think they're hoping you'll like it and decide to become a balloonist too. Come inside and meet them. I've called your mother, and everything is all set—if you want to go."

If he wanted to go! Doug could hardly believe it.

After good-byes and with promises to stop on their way back, Bruce, Lester, and Doug were on their way to the high school football field.

"Carl's on the field looking after our balloon," Bruce said. "Lester and I do the riding, and Carl takes care of the equipment and picks us up when we land."

At the football field, the balloon lay spread out on the ground, its stripes of blue and orange and yellow wrinkled and limp.

"Here, Doug. You can help us hold open this hole at the bottom of the balloon. Carl is going to start the engine, and its fan will blow air into the balloon." So Doug helped Lester and Bruce spread out the big opening at the bottom of the balloon, and, as the fan blew air into it, slowly the balloon began to fill until it was tall and round and huge as it hung over them with its dangling burner and basket.

"Hang on, Doug, keep hold of that basket," Lester yelled. "We don't want the balloon to get away from us. You go with him, Bruce, I'll stay with Carl. In you get, Doug," and Lester helped Doug scramble over the side of the basket. They floated upward. Then came a mighty roar, a tremendous whoosh, and Doug thought it was all over for him.

"I lit the burner," Bruce said. "It makes an awful noise while it is on. It sends hot air into the balloon through the opening which is just above it. The hot air expands and makes the balloon go higher. The balloon floats on air like a cork on water. The cork cannot go up and down, but a balloon can. Send hot air into it and up it goes. Let it cool and down it goes."

Now they were above the high school building, up over the town. Doug could look down and see the streets laid out in squares, the park, the winding river. Above the treetops, then down over a cornfield where a farmer was waving at them.

"Can you steer a balloon?" Doug asked.

"Somewhat," Bruce said. "You do it by going up and down to find different air currents and by watching which way the wind is blowing. But once in the balloon you don't really care where you're going—you just enjoy it. That's why Carl follows us with the car and picks us up where we land."

Now Doug was conscious of the deepest quiet he had ever known. There wasn't a sound anywhere as they floated. He felt a freedom, a lightness, a *peace* —that was the word that best described how he felt. It was different from anything he'd ever known. He'd tell Bruce he was going to be a balloonist!

"I'm sorry," Bruce said, "but we must land now. I think we can make that old airstrip. I see our car and another one following it."

"That's Dad's car," Bruce said, and he waved and called as they came down. Bruce had pulled a cord that opened a vent in the top of the balloon, and, with air going out, the balloon slowly settled onto the ground. As Doug scrambled out, Lester got in the basket.

"Thank you! Thank you! Good-bye and good luck in the race," Doug shouted as the balloon went up again.

"Well, I'll be on my way to Iowa," Carl said and drove off.

"I couldn't miss seeing you," Dad said. "Mother called me. How was it?"

"Just wonderful!" Doug tried to describe the ride. "What if I hadn't gone to Mrs. Hughes's today? Look what I'd have missed!"

"There won't always be a balloon ride for keeping a difficult promise," Dad said.

"I know. The balloon was great, but I'll always remember, too, how good I felt when I looked at the yard after I'd cleaned it up and Mrs. Hughes's smile as she thanked me."

> Finally, brethren, whatever is true, whatever is honorable, whatever is just . . . think about these things.
>
> Philippians 4:8 RSV

Dear God, I want to be a dependable person, one who keeps his promises, who can be trusted to follow through as Jesus did. Forgive me when I fail, but help me to keep on trying. Amen

The Jungle Gym

"All in favor of the playground project, raise their right hands," Tim directed, and glanced around the group. Yes, it was unanimous. Even pint-sized Oscar, taking his cue from the others, got that lopsided grin on his face and raised his hand. Tim snorted to himself. "I don't know why he keeps on showing up for Youth Fellowship. I'll bet he can't understand a single word that is said." Tim recalled himself to the duty at hand. "Then I'll notify the trustees of the church that we have voted to build a playground for the neighborhood kids on that lot in back of the church. I don't need to say, do I, that we'll spend their money carefully?"

"Plus do all the work," piped up Joe. Leave it to Joe.

Tim ignored him. "Now then, Terry, you say you and Mac know an officer of a construction company who will donate large ditch tiles to lay on the ground for a crawl-through? Can you call him tomorrow?"

"Sure."

"I found out that the city park department is replacing some of its swing equipment," volunteered Jane. "There's a possibility we can buy an old one cheap. I'll check into that."

"Good. It's shaping up already. As I said before, my dad and I will build the jungle gym. Dad has drawn up the plans and will order the wood this week. Are any of the rest of you handy with tools?"

Blank stares answered his question.

"OK, the two of us will manage. We could use some posthole diggers on Saturday. See you then." Tim banged the gavel. "Meeting adjourned."

Riding home on his bike, Tim thought with pride about the playground. This was the first big project the junior highs had undertaken for the church, and all the members were pitching in to do a thorough job. Even little Oscar. Tim sighed. What could they find for him to do? Trying to be fair, Tim realized it must be tough to be uprooted and put down in a strange country, away from your friends and everything familiar. Tim's church had offered to sponsor a Cuban refugee family, and the Lopezes had arrived about a month ago. They had been coming to church and were on a waiting list to attend English classes at the Hispanic Center. Tim had learned that Oscar had a tutor who interpreted for him at school. But it was really taxing, trying to communicate with someone who didn't speak your language. Tim certainly did not have the knack.

Saturday morning found the lot behind the church bustling like a Boy Scout Jamboree. A sandbox had been constructed underneath a spreading maple tree and was being filled with sand, Terry and Mac were putting together the swing set, and Jane and Oscar —Oscar?—were busy applying bright-colored paints to the ditch tiles. Tim watched them for a moment. They seemed to be getting along famously, with much giggling and exaggerated sign language.

Tim turned to help his father who was marking off spaces for the jungle gym with stakes and string. He consulted his drawings and measured carefully. "We're ready for those posthole diggers now," said Tim's father, straightening up.

Tim called several of his friends, and they set to work. Before long all the posts were in place and the jungle gym frame was beginning to rise. Tim could see Oscar looking at them intently now and then, almost forgetting to paint.

At noon everyone scattered to other activities, leaving Tim and his father—and Oscar—alone. Tim and his father sat down under the maple tree, opened their sack lunches, and motioned to Oscar. "I hope he likes peanut butter and jelly sandwiches," mumbled Tim as Oscar joined them. But Oscar had brought his own lunch. He spread a paper napkin carefully on the grass and unwrapped a plate on which lay several packets resembling small purses. "Oh," said Tim, brightening. "Tacos. I've eaten those at the Mexican restaurant here in town. They're good."

Oscar stopped with a taco halfway to his mouth.

He put it down and picked up the plate, holding it out to Tim. "Taco? Si?"

"Thanks, Oscar." Tim dredged up a word he had heard in the movies on television. "Gracias." He, in turn, held out a peanut butter and jelly sandwich to Oscar, who grinned from ear to ear.

"Gracias. Thank you."

"Hey, that's a beginning," returned Tim.

As they finished lunch, Tim's father announced, "I've got to make a trip to the lumberyard. Some of these boards need to be routed. I may be gone awhile. Can you go ahead, Tim, with the work? You might tackle building the ladder. I left the drawings under a rock on top of those two-by-fours. Perhaps you can find something for Oscar to do. He could probably bolt together those railing boards if you show him how to get started."

"Sure, Dad. Take your time. Come along, Oscar. Over here." Tim made a broad sweep with his arm and loped over to the jungle gym. Oscar followed.

Tim laid out the wood and screws for Oscar to use. He drilled a hole in both ends of a two-by-four board, then did the same with a second, securing the two boards together with a bolt and screw. "Now you do it," he told Oscar, passing him the drill. "You understand?"

Oscar nodded. "Si. Comprendo." A flood of Spanish engulfed Tim as he turned away.

Tim located the two upright posts for the ladder and the crosspieces. "I don't need the drawings," he muttered. "I've been building ladders since I was a kid." He dug around for a hammer and long nails.

67

"These ought to do nicely." Tim placed the uprights on the ground, spaced the crosspieces evenly, and started pounding nails. He had completed four rungs before he realized the drill had stopped buzzing. He looked up on the platform to find Oscar frowning at him. "What's the matter, Oscar? You're doing a fine job."

Oscar shook his head and jumped down beside Tim. He pointed at the ladder. "No, no. No es seguro. Házlo asi." Before Tim could stop him, Oscar picked up the hammer and began ripping nails out of the crosspieces.

"Hey, what do you think you're doing?" Tim demanded, grabbing the hammer away from Oscar.

Another flood of Spanish washed over him. There was no smile on Oscar's face now. He appeared quite determined. "No es seguro!" he shouted emphatically. Then, as Tim continued to stare, Oscar ran to pick up the drawings. Bringing them back, he pointed to a portion showing the outline of the ladder. "Házlo asi," he said, moving his finger around the sketch of the ladder.

Tim examined the drawing. "I see," he said slowly. "The drawing calls for the upright supports of the ladder to be notched out and the crosspieces fitted into them. I was doing it wrong. How did you know that, Oscar?"

For an answer, Oscar picked up a saw. Tapping Tim on the shoulder, he indicated a chisel and hammer. Oscar neatly sawed two slots in one of the upright ladder supports, then motioned to Tim to chip out the wood between the slots with chisel and hammer. In a sort of dream, Tim did so.

They were working on the last notch when Tim's father returned. "You two are quite a team," he remarked. "How did you teach Oscar so quickly, Tim?"

"I didn't teach him a thing, Dad. He taught me." Tim explained.

"That's interesting. Somewhere Oscar has learned a lot about woodworking. For instance, he knew that the ladder would not be strong and safe unless the rungs were set in, not nailed to the outside of the upright posts. It wouldn't last two months in that position. The posts must carry the weight, not the nails in the rungs. Any other design is dangerous."

"Dad, do you suppose Oscar's father likes carpentry work as much as you do? Maybe Oscar's father taught him, just the way you are teaching me." Tim pointed to his father and then to Oscar. "I wish I knew the Spanish word for carpenter." He repeated the gesture. "Carpenter?"

"Si, si." Oscar nodded enthusiastically. "Carpintero! Papa carpintero." He launched into another string of Spanish.

Tim laughed. "Cool it, Oscar. We'll need to continue this conversation after you've learned to speak English. Or I learn Spanish. I think I'd like that. Maybe this is a good time for me to start." He put his hand on his chest, then held it out to Oscar. "Friend," he said, pumping Oscar's arm.

Oscar's face lit up. "Friend. Amigo. Comprendo?"

"Comprendo!" Tim called to his father. "Hey, Dad, I'm learning Spanish from a pro. Oscar and I are amigos."

Let all that you do be done in love.

1 Corinthians 16:14 RSV

Dear Lord, teach me to be kind and loving to everyone I meet. Remind me that offering my friendship is important. Amen

Kevin Follows Through

Youth Newssheet
Bethany Church
Personals:
Marcia is off to Virginia;
Donald to Wilderness Camp;
Kevin Mason—Just wait
'till you hear about Kevin!

Kevin laughed out loud when he read the inside page of the newssheet:

Kevin Mason—Financier of the
backyard baby service. . . .

He'd get plenty of kidding about it, but it had been worth it! Kevin's face sobered as he remembered what had started it all.

"I finally got your father to see a doctor," his

mother had said. "We both know he's not been feeling well for some time. The doctor is putting him right in the hospital."

Packed and ready to go, Kevin's father had said, "I'll be back soon, Kevin. While I'm gone, look after your mother and Wesley."

But his father had not come home! He had died in the hospital.

Following the funeral, Kevin's mother had insisted they resume the same routine as before—but nothing was the same!

There had been school, his paper route, basketball practice. But Dad wasn't there to talk to about school or the problems on the route. He was no longer at the games where he had been an unofficial cheerleader for the team. On Sunday mornings, sitting with Mother in church, he missed Dad on the other side of him. And after church, Wesley came running down the hall from the nursery, always calling for "Daddy, Daddy."

Kevin wasn't sure what he thought about heaven, but his mother's firm conviction and faith that his father was safe and somewhere with God comforted him. What troubled him as the weeks went by was the remembrance of his father's words, "Look after your mother and Wesley." He wasn't doing a thing, though Mother said that just carrying on as cheerfully as possible was a tremendous help. But Kevin wanted to do something more!

Then last night his mother had said she was going to work. "Your father's illness was very expensive," she had said. "When Dr. Jamison called me and said the church secretary was leaving and would I like the position, I said yes. It's an answer to my prayers. I can walk to the church, leaving after you do in the morning. Wesley can stay in the church nursery school and will be very happy there. You can continue with your spring track practice, and I'll even be home before you.

"The only difficulty will be finding a baby-sitter for Wesley from three to five-thirty. The nursery school closes at three and I won't be through with work until five-thirty. And poor Wesley is terrified now when I leave him. I think he's afraid I won't return, like Father."

Getting ready for bed, Kevin thought of his father's words and realized that now he had an opportunity to follow through on them. He could take care of Wesley! It would mean giving up his paper route, the track team (and he was just beginning to be really good!), and not being with his friends. Could he do it? Day after day?

At breakfast he told his mother not to look for a baby-sitter. He had an idea of someone she could get. He thought of his idea all through school. That evening he said, "Mother, I'd like to volunteer as Wesley's baby-sitter. I get out of school on time to pick him up from the nursery. I can play with him in the backyard until you get home."

"Do you mean every day, Kevin? Have you thought of all you'll have to give up?"

"Yes, I mean every day," Kevin replied. "And I've really thought about it. You won't have to worry about Wesley, and he'll be happy. Besides," and he grinned, "think of the money you'll save by not having to hire a baby-sitter."

"It's a wonderful idea, Kevin. If you've thought it through carefully and realize what it will mean, we'll try it."

On the Monday his mother went to work for the first time, Kevin became Wesley's baby-sitter. As the days went by, he found it harder than he had expected. Rolling a ball back and forth, pushing the swing, playing in the sand, helping Wesley ride, answering his calls to "Play with me, Kevin," became less and less fun. "What he needs is someone his own age to play with," decided Kevin.

He told his mother his plan that evening. She took his announcement with her the next morning to be put in the church paper.

Baby-sitter for five-year-olds, Monday through Friday, 3:30 to 5:30 P.M. Fenced-in yard, playthings, good care. Call Kevin Mason at 861-2598 for an appointment. $1.00 an hour.

His idea had worked! Every day Wesley had had two or three friends to play with. Kevin became the supervisor, separating two children hanging onto the same toy, drying the tears of one with a scraped knee and bandaging it up, comforting another who suddenly wanted his mother. There was lots of activity, and the children were generally contented with each other, which gave Kevin time to practice his drawing.

One day he had made sketches of the children to show his mother. He had never done anything like it before and had found it great fun. His mother had been amazed and impressed and had shown the drawings to a friend who was an artist. Now Kevin was taking lessons from her. He had half a sketch book filled with his pictures of his new friends. And on Sunday mornings, Wesley and his friends came running down the hall calling "Kevin, Kevin."

There had also been another advantage to his plan that delighted Kevin. At the end of the first week, he had given his mother $13 earned from his baby-sitting. Together they had gone to the bank and opened a new joint account with both their earnings.

"We're partners in finance," his mother said, "but partners also in a much deeper sense. Your taking on the responsibility of caring for Wesley has made us all happier. I feel we're a whole family again. We'll never forget your father, but now we know that we can go forward together as he'd have wanted us to do. He'd be very proud of you, Kevin, as I am!"

That night as Kevin thought of his father, he seemed very near and very real. He prayed:

"Thank you, God, for helping me find a way to do what Dad wanted me to do. Keep me at it. Amen."

> A good name is to be chosen rather than great riches, and favor is better than silver and gold.
> Proverbs 22:1 RSV

Dear God, help me to understand that accepting responsibilities can lead to new opportunities. Open my eyes to the riches of your world and its creative possibilities. Amen

A Sure Foundation

"Either your dog is trained and learns to obey, or I'm afraid he'll have to go," Tom's father said as he held up a new tennis shoe ruined by Buffy's playing with it. Soon afterward Tom heard the front door shut as his father left for the office.

"What can I do, Mom?" asked Tom as he joined his mother and the twins at the breakfast table.

"Hi, Tom! Hi, Tom! Breakfus! Breakfus!" shouted the twins, Judith and Jerry, banging on their trays with their spoons.

"Hush! Judith, Jerry. Remember, we shout outdoors, but at the table we *talk*," Mother said, and the twins, not yet two, nodded in agreement.

"I've never trained a dog," Mother said. "It must be something the same as training the twins."

"Only we don't get rid of them when they don't behave," grumbled Tom.

Mother laughed. "That's right, but your father had reason to be upset. He wanted to wear those shoes this afternoon in the tournament. And that's the second pair Buffy has ruined. Ask your friends at school what they do. There must be some place you can get help."

At school, Tom's friends were not of much help. "Tell your dog what to do and hit him if he doesn't mind," seemed to be the general answer. But Tom knew he could never hit Buffy. You didn't hit anyone or anything you loved!

Saturday morning his church fellowship was having a paper collection to raise money for a trip to Indian Mound Park. Tom went early to the church to talk with Don Burton, the youth leader, about his problem.

"Yesterday I couldn't have helped you," Don said, "but this morning I can. I had breakfast with my brother this morning and told him about our paper drive. He offered to help us by giving five lessons in training dogs and donating the fees to our travel fund. He's had a training school before and is very good. He calls it the Canine Obedience School. I've arranged to have the school in the church gymnasium. It will start next Wednesday night. Think you can keep Buffy out of mischief until then?"

"Wow! That's great!" Tom said. "That's just what Buffy and I need. How can we help get it started?"

"I have four people interested, but we could use a few more."

"Buffy and I make five. Why can't we ask people when we get their papers today?" asked Tom.

"Of course. Good thinking, Tom."

78

Don explained the Canine Obedience School to the other boys as they gathered for the paper drive. All agreed it was a good idea and would help tell of it. At the end of the day they had five more customers for the school and $62.05 for their travel fund.

On Wednesday night, Father drove Tom and Buffy to the gym. "Have a good time, Tom," Father said. "And you be a good dog, Buffy, and learn your lessons. I'll be back in an hour."

Tom joined the people and their dogs going into the gym. They were told to sit on chairs placed in a circle, and to hold their dogs on a short leash.

Don introduced his brother, John, who said, "Why don't you and your dogs get up now, walk around a bit, but not too near one another, and I'll come around to meet you all." Tom and Buffy were glad to walk before sitting down again.

Then John gave instructions on the best ways to train dogs in obedience, stressing patience and kindness. Following that, they tried to put his teaching into practice by training their dogs to "heel" and to "sit" on command.

"Don't be discouraged," John said. "Practice every day with your dog until next Wednesday. See you then."

Tom's father was waiting. In the car Buffy snuggled down in Tom's lap and went to sleep. He had worked so hard in school!

"We're to get ice cream, Tom. Everyone is waiting to hear about Buffy and his school," Father said.

When they reached home, Tom tried to demonstrate what they had learned at school. But Buffy

neither "heeled" nor obeyed the command to "sit." Instead he ran in and out of the chairs, happy to be free and home again.

"I think he's making fun of you," Mother commented.

"He does look as if he might be laughing, but he'll learn his lessons, I'm sure," Father said.

"It will certainly help when we can tell Buffy to sit—"

"Look!" Father cried and pointed. There was Buffy sitting quite still and looking at Tom.

"Come," called Tom, and Buffy ran into his arms.

"You did learn, didn't you?" said Tom. "We'll give you an A for your first lesson."

"Good Buffy! Good Buffy!" shouted Jerry.

"Hush, Jerry! No shouting now. Outdoors!" said Judith.

"OK. Outdoors," said Jerry.

"We'll give you both an A too," laughed Mother as she kissed them and took them to bed.

"So even the twins can be trained," smiled Tom.

"Yes," said Father. "We all need training. But with us it's different. We can understand why we have to learn certain rules and ways of behavior. Animals can only obey. Remember how your mother says to the twins, 'We *talk* at the table.' She is giving them a reason for not shouting. People can understand why certain rules make it pleasanter to live together, why they help us develop into better people, the kind God planned us to be."

"You mean rules like the Ten Commandments?" asked Tom.

"Yes, those and the ones Jesus gave."

"You mean like 'Love your neighbor'?"

"Yes. Rules are the beginning. They are the foundation on which we build. If we follow them faithfully, eventually we don't think of them as rules because they have become a part of us. They help make us the kind of people who want to follow certain *principles,* as they are called. Then we can become the kind of people Jesus wanted us to be."

> Keep on loving one another as Christian brothers.
>
> Hebrew 13:1 TEV

Dear God, help me to learn and understand your rules so that I may become the loving person you would like me to be. Forgive me when I forget, and help me to try again. In Jesus' name, I pray. Amen

The Cameraman Doesn't Lie

Phil flipped through the pages of *Young Photographer*. "C'mere, Kenny," he shouted. "Look at this." Phil's younger brother bolted into the room from the kitchen and flung himself on the floor beside Phil.

"A contest," Phil went on, reading. "*Young Photographer* is holding a contest for all teenagers. First prize is your photo printed on a cover of the magazine and," he rolled the words around lovingly, "$100! Isn't that neat?"

Kenny pounded Phil on the back. "You could win, Phil, you really could. Your pictures are getting better all the time. Even Mr. Nelson says so, and he's an expert."

"Thanks. You don't do poorly yourself. But then, of course, you're not old enough to enter." Phil spoke with the loftiness of a 13-year-old. He read on, mumbling to himself. "Black and white . . . 8x10 glossy print . . . one entry per person . . . deadline. . . ."

A honking horn interrupted his reading. "Oops, there's my ride. See you later, Kenny." Phil grabbed up his camera and shot out the door. "Bye, Dad," he called to his father who stood visiting with Mr. Nelson, driver of the car. "We'll be back around three o'clock." Phil squeezed into the car with four other boys, and the car moved away from the curb.

Phil had looked forward all week to this Saturday. Mr. Nelson, his scoutmaster and owner of the neighborhood camera shop, had promised to take several of the troop's photography buffs on a camera safari to the city zoo.

Phil passed on the contest information he had uncovered, and the boys chattered excitedly about it all the way to the zoo. "You might find some interesting subject material here at the zoo," chimed in Mr. Nelson as he pulled into the parking lot.

"Sure," agreed Phil. "Everyone loves photos of animals." He dreamed of catching a lion in midroar or rolling on its back as he hung his camera around his neck and removed the lens cover. He headed straight for the lions' area, only to find two of his friends already there. They all snapped pictures of a handsome male lion sunning himself atop a huge rock, good-naturedly swapping knowledge about f-stops and shutter speeds with each other as they worked. When it appeared that old Leo was not going to budge from his rock for any spectacular movement, Phil wandered off to the giraffe pen. By patient waiting, he was rewarded with a picture of

84

a mother licking her baby and one of the baby nursing.

"I might have something special there," he told himself. Part of the excitement of photography for Phil was discovering a truly artistic print when he processed his film.

After stopping to shoot a snoozing tiger and a close-up of a camel's head, Phil looked around for more active subjects. His eyes lighted on the monkey cage the other side of a small picnic grounds. Monkeys were always fun material. First, though, he needed to put fresh film in his camera. As he sat down at a picnic table in the shade and bent over his task, his foot struck something solid on the ground. Leaning down, Phil found that someone had dropped a roll of black-and-white film. "Maybe it belongs to one of our guys," he reasoned, absently slipping the film in a jacket pocket with his own roll. "I'll ask on the way home."

All too soon the safari ended, and the group piled back in the car. Phil brought out the film he had picked up, but no one claimed it. He put it back in his pocket and forgot it, his thoughts moving ahead to his arrival at home. There would be just enough time for him to develop his pictures before dinner. Phil's heart beat faster. Would he find he had taken a possible contest winner? He hoped so, for he had decided exactly what to do with that $100 prize.

Hardly pausing to fill in his family about the trip, Phil clumped down to his basement darkroom. Hanging his jacket on a hook, he dug in a pocket for his film, his hand closing at the same time over the film he had retrieved from under the picnic table. He set the stranger's roll on the table. He could sympathize with the other photographer's loss. Tough luck.

Scrounging around in a cabinet, Phil found his black film-changing bag and began the first step in developing, winding his film on a spool inside the bag. His eyes strayed to the film on the table. What was on it? he wondered. There was no way he could ever find the owner. Should he develop the film? His can held two spools at a time for processing. Why not?

Phil whistled and thought again about what he would do with the prize money as he cycled the negatives through all the chemical washes. "I'll buy Dad that heavy-duty electric drill he's been wanting." Phil's father had a workshop in the garage. It had been handy for making repairs around the house. When he was little, his dad had built him and Kenny a wagon, and just last summer a wonderful tree house. Dad was always saying how much quicker he could finish jobs if he owned a heavy-duty electric drill. Well, before long he could have one. The idea of helping his father this way made Phil feel important and grown up.

He held the dried strips of negatives up to the light. The giraffes looked pretty good. The stranger's film, too, had been taken at the zoo. The shots were excellent, better than his own, Phil admitted, comparing them. He laughed aloud at a shot of the tiger sunk up to his neck in a pool of water. The photographer had captured an expression of supreme contentment spreading over the tiger's face. He would print that one.

Laying out the pictures he had printed, Phil inspected them critically. His mother giraffe licking her baby showed detailed depth of field and interesting shadows. But the unknown photographer's picture of the tiger was terrific—a definite contest winner, Phil conceded with a prick of jealousy. The photographer had caught that extra quality that conveys a message and brings a photograph to life. How he wished he had taken it. His picture of the tiger wasn't half as well done. Phil sat staring at the tiger in the pool, an idea forming in his mind. Why couldn't he send in this photo as his own entry? Everyone would believe he had taken it. Only one person in all the world would know this wasn't Phil's shot, and he or she couldn't be positive. Phil *had* taken a picture of the tiger. Before he could change his mind, he filled out the contest entry blank and prepared the photo for mailing. He would drop it in the mailbox on his way to school on Monday. Boy, would his dad be surprised in a few weeks.

Phil toyed with his food during dinner, but no one noticed. The rest of the family was busy helping Kenny choose photos for his ecology poster. The members of his class were supposed to draw pictures to illustrate their posters, but Kenny had asked his teacher if he could use photos he had taken. She said, "Yes, that would count as original work."

Phil started his homework. Going in Kenny's room to borrow some paper, Phil stopped short, gazing in unbelief at the poster propped on Kenny's desk. Pasted smack in the middle, with a caption about wild animals pruning trees, was Phil's photo of the mother and baby giraffes. "Kenny!" Phil exploded.

"What do you mean by passing off one of my photos as your own?"

Kenny cleared his throat uneasily. "I didn't think you'd mind, Phil. Honest. It's all in the family, isn't it? I need a picture of a wild animal to make my point. I don't have any wild animals in my photo collection. You don't mind, do you?"

"Yes, I do mind. That's being dishonest." Phil ripped off the picture and stormed back to his room with it, slamming the door.

He sat with the picture in hand for a long time, seeing nothing. Why was he so upset with Kenny? Wasn't he himself doing the same thing? Could it be because he knew it wasn't right?

Phil drummed his fingers on his desk. Finally he got up quietly and went down to his darkroom. Opening up the package, he removed the tiger picture and inserted the giraffe photo. He sighed. It didn't have as much appeal, but it was his own work. If it didn't win first prize, it might still win one of the lesser awards. Holding the tiger picture, Phil closed his eyes. "Thank you, God, for turning me back before it was too late."

Phil leaned over and pinned the tiger picture to his cork board. He would keep it there to remind him of how easy it was to make mistakes and of how God holds us back from sinning.

> No temptation has overtaken you
> that is not common to man. God
> is faithful, and he will not let you
> be tempted beyond your strength.
> 1 Corinthians 10:13 RSV

Thank you, Lord, for being there to strengthen me at those times when I am tempted to be less than honest. Amen

Raymond Sounds the Alarm

"Hey, Vince—Charlie," Raymond called as two boys came riding toward him on their bikes. "I got to slide down the pole at the firehouse."

Charlie circled up and down the driveway. Vince rested one foot on the curb and shifted his heavy newspaper bag. "When was this, Raymond?"

"Yesterday, I think, or last week. Our class went to visit a firehouse. I wore a fireman's hat and sat in the cab of the truck."

"That's neat."

"Will you stay and play with me? We can play tag or Old Maid."

"Not now, Raymond. Charlie and I must finish delivering our papers."

"Will you come back? I haven't told you the best part of the trip to the firehouse."

"It'll be dinner time then, Raymond. Maybe to-morrow. Bye."

"Dumb kid," exploded Charlie as he and Vince rode on down the street. "Can't keep track of the days in a week. Has to go to a special school."

"Don't be upset with him, Charlie. He likes you. And I enjoy talking to him. He's always so happy."

Raymond stood looking down the street after them. Then he skipped up the driveway to his house.

"What time is it, Mom?" he asked, opening the door.

"Almost four o'clock," she replied.

"And is today Wednesday?"

"Yes."

"Goody." Raymond scooped up his walkie-talkie and raced back outside. Pressing the button, he spoke into the microphone. "Red Fox, this is Buddy O. Are you there? Hello, hello. Red Fox, this is Buddy O." He waited. Silence. Then a crackling filled the line.

"Hello, Buddy O. This is Tim—er—Red Fox. You remembered to call, didn't you?"

"Sure. You said every Wednesday, whenever you could, you would tune in your police radio at four o'clock to Channel 14, and we'd talk. I wouldn't for-get that."

"Good for you. Did your class have fun at the fire station?"

"You bet."

"How old are you, Raymond?"

"I don't know, maybe 13. I'm as tall as Vince. He's 13. I must be 13."

"What kind of books do you read in your school?"

"Golden Books are the best. Why?"

"I saw a book about fire fighting you would like. I'll drop it off at your house soon."

"Thank you. You're a nice man."

"It's time for me to sign off now, Buddy O. I'll talk to you next Wednesday. Will you know when it's Wednesday?"

"Of course. That's the day I watch 'The Invisible Planet' on TV. This is Buddy O out."

Next Wednesday, Raymond and his mother walked over to visit Aunt Ellen. Raymond took along his walkie-talkie to show to her. All the way home, he kept asking his mother the time. He could hardly wait to call Tim. Finally Mrs. Brown became annoyed. "Raymond," she said firmly, "it is quarter to four. Please don't ask me again. I will let you know when it's four o'clock. I won't forget."

They stood at the door while Mrs. Brown fished in her purse for her house keys. "I know they're here somewhere," she muttered. But they weren't. "I must have left them on the table at Aunt Ellen's," she said at last. "We'll have to go back."

"But I want to talk to Tim, that is, Red Fox. Aunt Ellen's house is too far away for the walkie-talkie signal to carry," wailed Raymond. "Can't I sit on the steps and wait for you?"

"I don't believe that would be—"

A voice from behind interrupted. "Can I help you, Mrs. Brown? Hi, Raymond."

Mrs. Brown turned. "Hello, Vince. Yes. Would it be convenient for you to stay with Raymond while I go back to my sister's? I'm afraid I left my keys at her house. None of our neighbors are home during the day. Everyone works, so I can't phone my sister to bring the keys. I can be back in about 20 minutes."

"No problem, Mrs. Brown. You take as long as you like. Raymond and I will play hide and seek."

Mrs. Brown hurried off. Raymond ran around to the backyard. He knew just where he would hide— in the yew bushes beside the patio. But he didn't. Instead he stood staring at the sun porch of the house next door. Dark smoke filled the porch and curled out cracks around the windows. Through a door, Raymond could see an ugly red glow in the room beyond. He heard Vince's voice, "Here I come, ready or not!" And Vince came pounding around the house.

"What is it, Vince?" Raymond asked him, pointing to the porch. "Why does it look so funny?"

"Oh, my gosh. The house is on fire. We've got to do something, Raymond. You're sure no one is home there—or anywhere else in the neighborhood?"

Raymond shook his head.

"Then we'll need to run to my house to turn in the alarm. Come on. Hurry. It's a long way from here."

Raymond held back. "Wait, Vince," said Raymond, lifting up his walkie-talkie. "What time is it?"

"Who cares about time? Come on!"

But Raymond tugged at Vince's shirt. "If it's four o'clock, I can call my fireman friend. He'll know what to do."

Vince's eyes popped wide open. "That's positively brilliant, Raymond. You're not so slow. It's just

94

after four. Call your friend—and pray he's there. Go on, there's not a second to lose."

Raymond pressed the button on his walkie-talkie. Vince held his breath as the instrument squawked. Red Fox answered. "You boys go stand on the front sidewalk. Don't go near the house next door," he instructed, after Raymond explained. "I'm turning in the alarm right now. I'll see you in a few minutes."

The boys could hear the siren several blocks away, then suddenly the big red truck was panting to a stop. The fire chief's car arrived. He hustled out. The other fire fighters followed him around to the back of the smoking house, carrying equipment.

Raymond and Vince watched from the safety of Raymond's backyard. The fire fighters worked quietly and competently to put out the fire. Once Tim glanced up and waved to Raymond. "Thanks, a lot, Buddy O."

Mrs. Brown arrived home while the fire fighters were finishing up. She offered to call the neighbors at their work places to notify them of the fire.

The next afternoon Raymond and Vince sat on Raymond's front steps telling Charlie about the excitement of the day before. They heard the sound of a heavy truck and spotted a fire engine cruising along the street.

"That's odd," said Vince. "It's not blasting its siren. Must not be going to a fire."

The fire engine eased over to the curb directly in front of Raymond and Vince and Charlie. Tim grinned down at Raymond from the driver's seat. "Hi, Buddy O." He and one of the other firefighters jumped down from the truck as Mrs. Brown came running out of the house.

."We've got something for you," said Tim, pulling a stiff sheet of paper from an inside pocket. He read: "Citation for Raymond Brown. Raymond Brown is hereby commended for his prompt and efficient action in reporting a fire on June 6, thereby enabling fire fighters to quickly extinguish a blaze and prevent excessive damage to property. Raymond Brown is cited as a useful and important citizen of this community. Signed, James J. Bradley, mayor of the city of Coatesville."

All the fire fighters applauded as Raymond took the sheet of paper. "What does it mean?" he asked when Tim shook his hand.

"It means you're a hero," cried Charlie, slapping Raymond on the back. "You're somebody important."

Raymond eyed Tim. "Am I important?"

"Very important, Buddy O," Tim answered solemnly, as he swung back into his seat and the fire engine roared away from the curb.

> For everything created by God is good, and nothing is to be rejected if it is received with thanksgiving; for then it is consecrated by the word of God and prayer.
>
> 1 Timothy 4:4-5 RSV

Dear God, help us to appreciate all your people, and learn that each one of us is important in your kingdom. Amen

The Duck Connection

Ernie dug the sack of bread scraps out of his newspaper bag and trotted across the street to the grassy bank of the canal which flowed through the city. Spotting an elderly man a short distance up stream, surrounded by a cluster of noisy white ducks, Ernie joined him.

"Hi, Mr. Williams."

"Good afternoon, son," the man replied, eyeing Ernie's bag. "How's life in the newspaper world to-day?"

"Great, just great, Mr. Williams. I've got a few extra copies this week. Have one."

Ernie scattered his bread for the ducks to eat while Mr. Williams scanned the newssheet. "That's a well-written article about Saturday's Little League game. One of yours?"

"Yes, thank you." Ernie gently disengaged a curious duck nibbling at his pant leg. "My friend Mark helps me with the printing, but I do most of the writing in 'Timely Topics.' I love to write."

"It shows. What are you going to do with all this talent?"

"I'd like to be a reporter for a big newspaper or a television station. It would be kind of neat to have a million people listen every evening to what I had written. Maybe I'll be a television reporter."

"Well, you've still got some time to make up your mind. By the way, there's Susie at your pant leg again. She must think you're a particularly juicy plant."

"Shoo, Susie. Take this piece of bread." Ernie picked up a piece on the ground and held it out to the duck. "There don't seem to be as many ducks on the canal these days, Mr. Williams, only the white ones. Where have all the mallards and wood ducks gone?"

"Out to the country to forage for grain and other food in the fields. I'm worried about these domestic ducks with winter coming on. There's not enough food along the canal to keep them alive this winter. They're in danger of starving."

"Starving! Why don't they fly away to find food too?"

"They can't. They're too heavy to fly. The wings of domestic ducks are too weak to support them in the air."

"Then how did they get here on the canal in the first place?"

"People who owned them as pets brought them. This seemed a good place to turn them loose. And

at first it was. Only now that the flock has multi-
plied to around 50 or 60, all of them can't survive
through the winter on the available plants."

"They look so plump. I can hardly believe they
will starve. But you should know. You used to work
for the conservation department, didn't you?"

Mr. Williams nodded.

"We've got to do something, Mr. Williams. We
can't let the ducks starve without trying to help
them. They're a part of God's world too. Do you
think if we asked all our friends to bring bread
every day that would save them?"

"Bread's not heat-producing enough for freezing
weather. They need seeds and grain." Mr. Williams
stuffed his empty bread sack in a jacket pocket and
turned to leave. "If you have any ideas, let me know,
Ernie. I'm very fond of these ducks, and I know
you are too."

"Sure. Bye, Mr. Williams." Ernie pulled up his
coat collar against the brisk wind and headed home.

As he entered the house, the smell of his favorite
stew filled the air, and he could hear the muffled
sounds of his mother's dinner preparations. Dad was
just turning on the TV set in the family room. Although his mother privately disapproved of TV with
meals, Dad liked to catch up on what had happened
in the city during the day while he was at the office.
So the family watched the local news while they ate.
Ernie slid into his place. Usually he studied carefully the newscaster's style, thinking about his own
future. Glen Johnson was certainly good, as good as
any of the national newscasters in Ernie's opinion.

But tonight he just half-listened, his mind circling around the problem of the ducks on the canal.

As soon as he finished dinner, Ernie went down to his basement "newsroom." He sat down at the ancient typewriter one of his dad's friends had given him. Ernie looked around his "office" at the stacks of paper, at his neat files, at the rotary printing press his parents had bought him. They had encouraged him to publish his weekly "Timely Topics." And the neighbors seemed to enjoy reading his strictly personal slant on happenings up and down their street. He now had 47 customers paying 15 cents a copy and the promise of more. Ernie tipped back in his chair. He liked to start thinking about his lead article for the next issue as soon as the previous one had been delivered. He mumbled to himself. "Mrs. Grimes gives birth to twins—no, everyone knows that. Dan Snyder wins regatta for 'Snipe' class—no, let's see. . . ." After a minute Ernie sucked in his breath loudly and let his chair hit the floor hard. "That's it!" he crowed, banging the desk with his fist. "I'll put out an 'extra' at no charge to my customers."

"Dad," he called, bounding up the stairs two at a time, "I want to ask you something. Is there anything wrong with soliciting funds through my 'Topics'?" He explained about the ducks. "If I can get some of my customers to donate money, Mr. Williams and I can buy sacks of corn to feed the ducks every day during the cold months. Maybe some of our neighbors would even help with the feeding. I'm sure Mark would."

"That would be okay, Ernie. Just be sure to state

that the money will be placed in a bank account and used for this purpose only. You can report on the response in future issues. It's a good plan."

Ernie raced back to the basement. He would alert Mark to come over right after school tomorrow. He shoved a sheet of paper in the typewriter. He already knew the headline. "Save Our Starving Ducks," he wrote. "According to a noted conservation expert, . . ." Ernie became absorbed in writing.

"It's not working," he announced anxiously to his father a few evenings later as he came in for dinner. "Counting the $5 you gave me, I've collected only $18. That won't feed the ducks for more than one week. We've got to have commitments for more than a week."

"Let me take a few of your 'Topics' to the office, Ernie. I'm certain some of my co-workers will contribute."

"Thanks, Dad. I wish I could dream up some way to let the whole city know. There must be lots of people who would donate money to save the ducks, if only they knew about the problem. Hundreds of people drive along the canal every day. They have no idea the ducks are hungry." Ernie reached out and switched on the TV set. The six o'clock news was just beginning. He flopped down on his stomach to watch Glen Johnson. Ernie noted again how sincere and convincing the newscaster appeared, the kind of person you could believe in. Suddenly Ernie bolted upright.

His father stared. "What's the matter, son?"

"I've just hatched the most brilliant brainstorm of the century, that's all. Where's a stamp? And an envelope? When is the last mail pickup in this area?" Ernie pounded to the basement and started typing. His father shook his head and turned back to the news.

Next morning, a Saturday, Ernie hung around the house, to the concern of his parents. "Aren't you going to play tennis at the 'Y'?" his mother asked. "You're giving up the bike hike this afternoon?" queried his father. Ernie just shrugged and tried to look interested in a book.

At 11:58 A.M. the phone rang. Ernie dashed for it, but his father was there first. "It's for you," he stated, holding out the phone, a puzzled expression on his face. "Some man says his name is Glen Johnson."

Ernie reached for the instrument with shaking hands. "Hello."

"Ernie, this is Glen Johnson at station WWPR. I received your letter and copy of your newspaper, 'Timely Topics.' I wanted to tell you that we have checked out your story, and the station intends to help the ducks. We'll run an item on the evening news tonight. We plan to set up a 'Feed the Ducks Fund' to receive donations. I think I can promise you that enough money will come in to guarantee food all winter for the ducks. People like to get behind a community project like this when it's brought to their attention. Those ducks won't starve. Later on, if the account gets low, we'll run another appeal on the air. Now here's what we'd like to do. Can you meet me and a cameraman at a point on the canal near you this afternoon? I'd like to interview you and get a few shots of the ducks. OK?"

Ernie's voice came out in a whispered croak, "OK."

"It'll be a good feature, lots of local color. See you later. Good-bye."

Ernie hung up the phone and collapsed on a chair. In a minute he would call Mr. Williams with the good news. But first he'd catch his breath—and tell his folks. "Hey, Dad," he shouted, a grin splitting his face. "Guess what?"

> Thou hast given him dominion
> over the works of thy hands;
> thou hast put all things under
> his feet.
>
> Psalm 8:6 RSV

Dear God, help me to look after the creatures in your world. Let me learn that along with enjoying them, I need to take responsibility for caring for them. Amen

Question and Answer

"What I want to know is how they became what they were so that we call them heroes?"

Gene asked the question during the Sunday school class discussion of their trip to Washington, DC. They had been home a week and Larry Hughes, their teacher, had begun the class with the question:

"What is the lasting impression or memory you will have of our trip?"

There had been many replies: fun, being with another youth group, making new friends, the city, talking with their senator. When it was Gene's turn, he said he agreed with all the replies but he was most impressed with the memorials and statues of the great men of their country: the Washington Monument, the Jefferson Memorial, the Tomb of the Unknown Soldier, and especially Lincoln's statue. "When we stood there looking up at him it was as if he could talk with us—with me, anyway. Did any of the rest of you feel like that?"

Several of his classmates nodded.

"He looked so sad, sort of, and so thoughtful. I wished I could ask him how we could—what we could do to become like him. Not that I want to be a hero (at this Gene's face became as red as his hair), but how we could learn to be ready to serve, not only our country but people, and be loved as he was."

A silence followed Gene's statements, for his classmates were surprised. Gene had never talked much, and never about himself.

"That's an excellent question, Gene," Larry Hughes said. "It's one we should all consider. This week, suppose each of us tries to find one way in which we can prepare ourselves for service to others in the pattern of the heroes Gene mentioned."

Class time was over, and they all clattered down the stairs. This was a special Sunday with a picnic on the church grounds. Families stayed after church for volleyball, races, and shared picnic lunches. Gene's class was responsible for setting up the volleyball net, so he and his friends rushed to the game closet. They found the net and supports and ran to the big front lawn and set them up. People were waiting and a noisy, happy group of adults and children were soon slapping the ball back and forth. Gene waved to his mother and father sitting with friends under a shady tree, then began playing.

A half hour later, hot and thirsty, he gave up his place to one of the waiting boys. He went in search of lemonade and found it in the church kitchen.

Inside it could be kept cool until it would be brought outdoors for lunch. Taking a paper cup, he served himself, sipping slowly and enjoying the coolness sliding down his throat. Now he was ready to enter the game again.

Going out the door, he thought he heard someone in the next room. He called out, but no one answered. Anxious to play ball again, he started down the hall, then stopped. Suppose there was someone in the room—like burglars. The church had been broken into just three weeks before. He should find out.

Slowly, walking on tiptoe, he returned to the kitchen and crept through it to the door of the next room. He reached around the door frame and snapped on the lights. With a sigh of relief he saw a very small girl with tears running down her cheeks huddled in a chair in the corner. Gene had never seen her before, and he thought he knew all the church members. Perhaps she was a visitor for the picnic.

"Hello," he said and sat down near her. "What's the matter?"

"I'm losted," she said and began crying with noisy sobs. "And everybody's gone."

Gene moved nearer and patted her shoulder. "I'm here," he said. "How did you get lost?"

"Mother got losted and I tried to find her," and the tears quivered on her cheeks as hiccups mixed with her sobs.

"Don't cry anymore," Gene said. "I'll help you find your mother. What's your name?"

"Holly."

"Holly what?"

"Holly dear," and with that Gene had to be content.

"Come on," he said. "We'll go outside and find your mother. I'll bet she's looking for you. Let's go." Taking her hand, Gene helped her off the chair. He started to walk, but Holly stopped and held up both arms to be picked up. "How tiny she is!" Gene thought as he lifted her into his arms.

"Momma's lost," she whispered.

"Nobody's lost now," Gene said. "Your mother is right outside looking for you." He walked down the hall with Holly's arms and her wet cheek pressed against his neck. Again he marveled at how tiny she was. No wonder she was frightened. The church rooms and halls must seem huge to her.

Holding her gently and carefully, Gene walked into the sunshine of the church yard, filled now with people. He went from group to group but no one knew Holly, and she clung more tightly to Gene, wetting his shirt with her tears. They had just about made the circuit of the yard when a woman came running from the children's playground.

"Holly, dear," she called. "I've been looking everywhere for you. Where have you been?" As the woman ran she held out her arms and, as she neared Gene, Holly jumped from his arms into those of her mother's.

"I was losted. But he found me." She pointed to Gene.

"Where did you find her?" she asked Gene.

Gene told her, then started to leave for the volleyball game. He hoped it wasn't all over. He was very glad Holly had found her mother. She sure was cute now that she was smiling.

"Wait a minute," Holly's mother said. "I haven't thanked you. And I'd like to know your name."

"Well, I'm Gene Albright, and I'm glad I could help Holly."

"I do thank you! We've been to church here for just two Sundays. I'm Mrs. Goodson, and I'll look forward to seeing you again. I'm sure Holly will also."

"Good-bye, Holly," Gene said. Holly leaned over to give him a quick hug from the security of her mother's arms.

That night, as Gene and his parents were reviewing the events of the day, the telephone rang. "It's for you, Gene," his father said.

"Gene, this is Mrs. Goodson. I want to thank you again for taking such good care of Holly. All she talks of is you. You're a hero to her—and to me as well. You saved her from an experience that could have left her frightened of the church so she would not have wanted to return there. Instead she knows there is someone there who cares for her and rescued her. Because of you, the church embodies the spirit of Christ. We are most grateful. Good-bye, Gene."

"Good-bye, Mrs. Goodson," said Gene. He hung up the receiver, then sat for some time looking at the telephone. He had been called a *hero*. A hero because he'd followed One who didn't have a statue in Washington. Someone who was better than any other hero and who said he wanted only to help others.

Here was a call to action he could begin to follow right away—not to become another hero, but because it had been wonderful to know that he had helped Holly to smile instead of cry.

> And Jesus increased in wisdom and in stature, and in favor with God and man.
>
> Luke 2:52 RSV

Dear God, help me to grow as Jesus grew. May I become aware each day of the things I can do to help others when they are in trouble or just to help make them happier because they know someone cares about them. Forgive me when I forget. Amen